+HB99.7 .K38 P54 1978

```
            Pigou, A. C. (Ar-
HB          thur Cecil), 1877-
99.7        1959.
K38
P54            Keynes's General
1978        theory
```

DATE DUE

```
            Pigou, A. C. (Ar-
HB          thur Cecil), 1877-
99.7        1959.
K38
P54            Keynes's General
1978        theory
```

DATE	ISSUED TO

REPRINTS OF ECONOMIC CLASSICS

KEYNES'S 'GENERAL THEORY'

KEYNES'S 'GENERAL THEORY'

A Retrospective View

BY

A. C. PIGOU

AUGUSTUS M. KELLEY · PUBLISHERS
FAIRFIELD 1978

First edition 1950
(London: Macmillan & Co., Ltd., 1950)

Reprinted 1978 by

AUGUSTUS M. KELLEY · PUBLISHERS
Fairfield, New Jersey 07006

By arrangement with Macmillan & Co. Ltd.

Library of Congress Cataloging in Publication Data

Pigou, Arthur Cecil, 1877-1959.
   Keynes's General theory.

    (Reprints of economic classics)
    Reprint of the 1950 ed. published by Macmillan, London.
Comprises two lectures given in Cambridge in Nov. 1949.
    1. Keynes, John Maynard, 1883-1946. The general
theory of employment, interest and money. I. Title.
[HB99.7.K38B54   1977]   330.15'6   76-57702
ISBN 0-678-01225-3

MANUFACTURED IN THE UNITED STATES OF AMERICA

PREFACE

THIS short book comprises two lectures given in Cambridge in November 1949 at the request of the Special Board for Economics and Politics for students in the Faculty. It is thus not intended for readers with no knowledge of Economics. Where, however, the argument is in essence mathematical, it has been translated into words. The lectures are printed as they were given with a few minor adjustments.

A. C. P.

KING'S COLLEGE, CAMBRIDGE
May 1950

CONTENTS

	PAGE
I. PRELIMINARY	1
II. THE MAIN PURPOSE OF THE 'GENERAL THEORY'	3
III. FULL EMPLOYMENT	5
IV. INCOME, SAVING AND INVESTMENT, THE STOCK OF MONEY AND THE RATE OF INTEREST	8
V. THE FUNCTIONS	12
VI. KEYNES'S FUNDAMENTAL CONCEPTION	20
VII. CONDITIONS NECESSARY TO THE KEYNESIAN EQUILIBRIUM	21
VIII. THE CHARACTER OF THE KEYNESIAN EQUILIBRIUM	25
IX. DIFFERENCES BETWEEN SHORT-PERIOD EQUILIBRIUM SITUATIONS	29
X. DIFFERENCES IN THE DEMAND SCHEDULE FOR INVESTMENT	31
XI. DIFFERENCES IN THE SUPPLY SCHEDULE FOR INVESTMENT	39
XII. DIFFERENCES IN THE LIQUIDITY PREFERENCE SCHEDULE	45
XIII. DIFFERENCES IN THE STOCK OF MONEY	47
XIV. DIFFERENCES IN THE MONEY-RATE OF WAGES	48

		PAGE
XV.	COMBINED DIFFERENCES	51
XVI.	EXPECTATIONS	53
XVII.	THE STATE AND INVESTMENT	57
XVIII.	LIMITATIONS AND ACHIEVEMENTS OF KEYNES'S ANALYSIS	61
XIX.	CONCLUSION	67
	APPENDIX	69

I

PRELIMINARY

SOON after Keynes's *General Theory* (1935) appeared, I wrote a review article about it in *Economica*. A part of that article was concerned with what seemed to me misrepresentations of things that other people had written; and this gave a controversial tone to it. Now, a decade and a half later, I should like to attempt an appraisement, as objective as I can make it, of what, apart from many secondary contributions, with which he adorned it, the book accomplished constructively. Keynes himself sincerely believed that it accomplished a great deal; and a large body of economists, as also of journalists who write about economics, at the present time agree with him. We frequently read of "the Keynesian revolution". Indeed, Keynesianism, or perhaps I should rather say Keynesianism without tears — for how many Keynesians, or, for that matter, anti-Keynesians either, have seriously studied his own book? — Keynesianism with-

PRELIMINARY

out tears is in danger of becoming a new orthodoxy. He himself, with his ever-exploring mind, would not have liked that. He would greatly have preferred a critical commentary.

II

THE MAIN PURPOSE OF THE 'GENERAL THEORY'

It is best, I think, to begin by setting out in his own words the main purpose of the *General Theory*. The analytical apparatus developed in it is explicitly designed to deal with problems of fluctuations over short periods. Thus in chapter 18, where his argument is summarised, Keynes writes : " We take as given the existing skill and quantity of available labour, the existing quality and quantity of available equipment, the existing technique, the degree of competition, the tastes and habits of the consumer, the disutility of different intensities of labour and of the activities of supervision and organisation, as well as the social structure, including the forces, other than our variables set forth below, which determine the distribution of the national income. This does not mean that we assume these factors to be constant ; but merely that, in this place and context, we are not considering or taking into account the effects and consequences of changes in them " (p. 245). These restricting assumptions exclude from consideration the consequences of a gradual increase in the stock of capital equipment consequent on successive investments made over a series of years. Thus questions about the ultimate equilibrium, if there is one, to which the whole creation moves, cannot be treated directly by Keynes's apparatus; though, as will be seen presently, they can in some measure be treated by it indirectly.

III

FULL EMPLOYMENT

NEXT, since Keynes's whole work is centred about the concept of full employment, it is important to get our notions about that clear. Most people by this time understand that he used this phrase in a peculiar sense. He did not mean by it, as the words in their natural sense imply, a state of things in which the number of persons actually employed is equal to the number of would-be employees. He meant by it this latter number minus 'frictional unemployment' associated with imperfections of mobility. It will be convenient to follow his usage here subject to an emendation. I shall regard employment as full when the number of persons actually employed is equal to the number of would-be employees minus frictional unemployment *and when there are no unfilled vacancies* (except frictional unfilled vacancies).[1] When the number of persons actually employed

[1] Frictional unemployment and frictional unfilled vacancies must, of course, always be equal.

is equal to the number of would-be employees minus frictional unemployment, and there *are* unfilled vacancies (over and above frictional unfilled vacancies), I say that there is *over-full* employment; the degree of over-fullness being measured by the number of unfilled vacancies other than frictional ones.

This distinction between full and over-full employment has no significance when we are enquiring into the effects of causes that tend to make employment larger. Their tendency is nullified equally whether in the initial situation employment is full or over-full. But with causes that tend to make employment smaller it has significance. If employment is simply full, their tendency is not nullified or, indeed, obstructed at all. On the other hand, if employment is over-full, it is obstructed to the extent of the over-fullness. With a cause tending to reduce employment by 100, if employment was initially over-full by 60, it will actually be reduced by 40. With employment initially over-full by 100 or more than 100, the tendency of employment to contract will be nullified. In the high tide of war and its immediate aftermath it may well happen that employment is sufficiently over-full to prevent any non-frictional unemployment from occurring as the result of any degree of any change that could reasonably be looked for.

What I have said so far is well enough for practical purposes. But for formal analysis it is necessary to measure employment and unemployment more exactly than by simply adding up the number of employed and of unemployed persons. Keynes uses for a measure a labour unit, in the sense of a unit of ordinary labour; labour that is paid, for example, twice as high as ordinary labour being counted as two labour units (p. 41). In so far as the relative rates of pay of different varieties and grades of labour remain constant, labour can be 'made homogeneous' by this device without any awkwardness. But, in so far as that condition is not satisfied, the same index number problem that hampers the measurement of changes in real income has to be faced — or ignored.

IV

INCOME, SAVING AND INVESTMENT, THE STOCK OF MONEY AND THE RATE OF INTEREST

WE come now to certain other important quantities that have to be defined, namely income, saving and investment, the stock of money and the rate of interest. A word or two must be said about Keynes's use of each of these words.

First, income. He distinguishes between income and net income. In reckoning income he makes a deduction from gross output to offset wear and tear of capital undergone as a result of use, but no other deduction. For net income he also makes a deduction to offset involuntary but not unexpected depletions of capital, such as losses through lapse of time irrespective of use and normal obsolescence (p. 51). Thus his 'net income' is substantially the same as Marshall's 'income'. It does not greatly matter which terminology we adopt; so long as we remember that, if we call Marshall's income net income, we must also call his investment and saving net investment and net saving. In what follows I shall adopt Marshall's usage and drop the 'net' before each of these words.

Secondly, saving and investment. As regards these, Keynes's usage in the *General Theory*, which is different from that followed in his *Treatise on Money*, is in conformity with 'classical' practice. Income is constituted of consumption plus investment. Saving is what remains of income when consumption is subtracted from it. Hence investment in the aggregate and saving in the aggregate are necessarily equal to one another; though there is no need for every or, indeed, for any individual person's investment to be equal to the saving made by him.

Thirdly, the stock of money. This, of course, for Keynes includes bank money (plus overdraft facilities), not merely currency, in circulation.

In the main part of his discussion he expresses and measures all the above quantities in terms of wage-units, *i.e.* the money wage-rate of a unit of ordinary labour. Evidently income expressed in this way, since it consists of money income divided by the money-rate of wages, is simply the labour value of money

THE STOCK OF MONEY

income — income valued in labour. Parallel meanings belong to investment, consumption and the stock of money in terms of wage-units. Keynes's usage here is logically watertight. But I myself find it troublesome, especially when we have to discuss money wage-rates. I shall, therefore, employ the phrase ' valued in labour ' instead of ' expressed in wage-units '. A further point should be noted. On occasions Keynes wants to refer to the stock of money, not in terms of wage-units, but in terms of money-units. On these occasions he sometimes makes his meaning clear by writing in brackets, after 'the stock of money', 'in terms of wage-units ' when he intends that, and writing ' the quantity of money as determined by the action of the central bank ' when he intends the quantity of money in terms of money-units (p. 247). But he does not always do this. Sometimes he refers to the quantity of money without saying explicitly whether he means quantity measured in wage-units or measured in money-units. When, as on page 173, his intention is obvious from the context, this does not matter. But sometimes, as we shall see, his usage threatens confusion.

Finally, the rate of interest. Keynes uses this term to represent ' the complex of rates of

THE RATE OF INTEREST

interest' and does not discuss the difficulties connected with movements of different rates relatively to one another. A further step might perhaps be taken if we were to operate with *two* representative rates, one short and one long.

V

THE FUNCTIONS

ALONGSIDE these various quantities Keynes brings into account the following functions.

First, there is the investment demand schedule, that is to say, the list of quantities of investment valued in labour that are demanded in respect of a corresponding list of rates of interest (compare p. 137). Keynes has an elaborate and excellent discussion of this under the name of the "schedule of marginal efficiencies of capital". The essential point is that, in a given state of expectations, a larger quantity of investment valued in labour is demanded, other things being equal, the lower is the rate of interest. That is to say, the quantity of investment demanded is a decreasing function of the rate of interest.

But there is a difficulty here. Keynes holds that the quantity of investment demanded is also an increasing function of the volume of consumption. He bases this view on the fact that capital goods are ultimately required only

THE FUNCTIONS

as a means to consumption, including, of course, consumption of services in the widest sense. Hence he writes : " Every weakening in the propensity to consume, regarded as a permanent habit, must weaken the demand for capital as well as the demand for consumption " (p. 106). This, in my opinion, is wrong. When consumption is *in process of increasing* there is, indeed, a consequential demand for investment to provide new equipment. But in situations of short-period equilibrium consumption must be regarded as fixed. True, when it is large, more expenditure has to be undertaken to make good wear and tear, and so on, than when it is small. But this expenditure does not come out of income ; for income is always reckoned *after* allowance has been made for it. Therefore it is not investment. It follows that, as between situations in short-period equilibrium investment is not an increasing function of — indeed does not depend at all on — the volume of consumption. This point will be found presently to be important.

His second functional relationship Keynes calls the propensity to consume. This is the list of quantities of consumption valued in labour that, in given conditions, the community will undertake corresponding to various quanti-

THE FUNCTIONS

ties of income, also so valued, that it is enjoying. This function is an increasing function ; characterised by the property that any given addition to income is associated with an increase in consumption, certainly smaller absolutely, and probably also smaller proportionately, than itself. This, it should be noted, is not incompatible with larger employment being associated with a larger proportion of total income going to wage-earners and with this making *pro tanto against* saving. But it is incompatible with that indirect reaction being dominant over the direct one.

Keynes holds that in general, with a given income, the amount of consumption is only affected very slightly by any variations in the rate of interest that are practically likely to occur. But he does not hold that it is altogether independent of the rate of interest. Indeed, as we shall see presently, when the rate of interest is only slightly above zero a cut in it to slightly below zero would make income and consumption equal. He prefers, however, to regard the propensity to consume as a function of one variable only, namely income (as valued in labour), the form of the function being liable to vary as the rate of interest varies, rather than as a function of two variables, income as above defined *and* the rate of interest. He is, of course, quite entitled to do this. But, since in two other of his functional relations the rate of interest appears as a variable within the function, it is inconvenient, when we want to co-ordinate the three of them, that in one it should appear in a different guise. I shall, therefore, emend Keynes's formulation here, putting the rate of interest within the function. Furthermore, I shall suppose, with Marshall, that with a given income (as valued in labour) consumption falls as interest rises; at the same time agreeing with Keynes that, income being given, variations in consumption due to the sort of variations in the rate of interest that are practically likely to occur will in general be small.

Before passing away from this function I must refer to a rather deep-reaching criticism which I have heard made in regard to it. It has been suggested that, since aggregate investment and aggregate saving are so defined that they must be equal to one another, the propensity to consume — and so the propensity to save — cannot be a psychological function depending simply on income and the rate of interest; it is tied up by definition with something else. This is, I think, a confusion.

Aggregate saving is, indeed, by definition always equal to aggregate investment. But it is only in conditions of equilibrium that the amount that people *desire to save* is equal to the amount that they and other people *desire to invest*. In disequilibrium the desired amount of saving and the desired amount of investment are not equal; there is a gap between them. An analogy may make this plain. The aggregate quantity of tea bought and the aggregate quantity sold must by definition be equal; just as the number of heads and tails on a bunch of pennies must be equal. This does not prevent the quantity of tea that people desire to sell being a psychological function of the price. The quantity actually sold is inexorably tied to the quantity actually bought. But the list of quantities which, at various prices, people desire to sell is not tied to anything.

Thirdly, there is the liquidity preference schedule or function. According to the Marshallian tradition, long current orally and set out in print in Part I, chapter 4, of *Money, Credit and Commerce*, people balance the marginal advantage of holding real resources respectively in the form of productive capital and in the form of money; the one advantage consisting in the prospective material yield (in the form of interest), the other in the yield of convenience and so forth. Thus, with real income given, the quantity of real resources held in the form of money, that is to say, the real value of the existing stock of money, is a decreasing function of the rate of interest. With real income not taken as given it is a reasonable approximation to regard the *proportion* of real income held in the form of money as a function, again, of course, a decreasing function, of the rate of interest.[1] This function we may call, if we like, the Marshallian liquidity preference function. Evidently the extent of liquidity preference associated with any given rate of interest is the inverse of the income velocity of money associated with that rate. If, with Keynes, we are to speak of money income measured in wage-units rather than of real income, that is to say, of the labour value, instead of the commodity value, of money income, no difference is made. For, if one-tenth or any other assigned fraction of income measured in commodities is held in the form of money, this implies that the same fraction of income measured in labour is so held. Keynes's intention, I have no doubt, is to make his liquidity preference function the same as the Marshallian one. Thus on page 167

[1] Cf. *The Veil of Money*, p. 83.

THE FUNCTIONS

he speaks of the rate of interest as "the price which equilibrates the desire to hold wealth in the form of cash with the available quantity of cash ". Elsewhere, however, he writes (p. 168): "Liquidity preference is a potentiality or functional tendency which fixes the quantity of money which the public will hold when the rate of interest is given"; and again, on page 171, he speaks of "the schedule of liquidity preference relating the quantity of money to the rate of interest". In their natural meaning these last two sentences are, to put it baldly, nonsense. For obviously the quantity of money that people hold must also, whatever the rate of interest, be exactly equal to the quantity that there is; and, since he has just been speaking of 'the quantity of cash', certainly in the natural meaning, the reader can hardly help supposing at first sight that the natural meaning is also intended here. If, however, we allow Keynes to intend by quantity of money in these two sentences quantity of money in terms of wage-units, that is, the labour value of the existing stock of money, all is well. What he is saying then agrees with what he said in the other passage quoted; and his liquidity preference schedule, subject to income being measured in labour instead of commodi-

THE FUNCTIONS

ties, is the same as Marshall's. Liquidity preference then is a decreasing, and the income velocity of money, which is the inverse of it, an increasing function of the rate of interest.

VI

KEYNES'S FUNDAMENTAL CONCEPTION

With the quantities and functions that I have been describing Keynes sets out his fundamental conception as follows: "Thus we can sometimes regard our ultimate independent variables as consisting of (1) the three fundamental psychological factors, namely, the psychological propensity to consume, the psychological attitude to liquidity and the psychological expectation of future yield from capital assets, (2) the wage-unit as determined by the bargains reached between employers and employed, and (3) the quantity of money as determined by the action of the central bank; so that, if we take as given the factors specified above, these variables determine the national income (or dividend) and the quantity of employment" (pp. 246-7). This summary statement contains, as I think, Keynes's main and very important contribution to economic analysis. I therefore want to emphasise it now. If I wasn't afraid that you'd feel insulted, I should read it over again!

VII

CONDITIONS NECESSARY TO THE KEYNESIAN EQUILIBRIUM

IN considering the conditions necessary to the Keynesian equilibrium, we see at once that he has left a gap. To make his analysis complete, he ought also to have included a physical factor, namely, the function relating the quantity of labour at work to the quantity of income (valued in labour) that is due to it. That function is obviously an increasing one, output increasing with employment, but increasing at a diminishing rate as employment increases. Let us suppose that this gap is made good.

Then for the system to be in equilibrium the following conditions must be satisfied:

(i) The quantity of resources which people demand for investment, depending on their expectations of future yields from capital assets, is equal to the quantity actually invested.

(ii) The quantity of resources (valued in labour) that people are willing to supply for investment, depending on the psychological propensity to consume, is equal to the quantity actually invested.

(iii) Money income is equal to the stock of money multiplied by the income velocity of money, which depends on a psychological attitude to liquidity in conjunction with the rate of interest.

(iv) Income valued in labour is equal to a given physical function of the quantity of labour at work, that is to say, of employment.

(v) The money-rate of wage is equal to money income divided by income valued in labour.

Over against these five equations we have seven unknowns; namely, employment, income in terms of money, income and investment, both of them valued in labour, the money-rate of wages, the rate of interest and the physical stock of money.[1] These unknowns will not be determined until two further independent equations have been introduced, bringing their number also up to seven.

One way in which these extra equations can be provided is exemplified in Marshall's *Principles*. For the purposes of that book, which dealt in the main with long-period tendencies,

[1] I use the phrase 'physical stock of money' as short for stock of money measured in terms of money-units. I apologise for making bank balances 'physical', but cannot think of a better word.

Marshall postulates that in equilibrium employment is always equal to the available labour force, and so, apart from changes in the number and age distribution of the population (together with another small qualification to be mentioned presently),[1] is fixed; there is always precisely full employment in Keynes's sense. This postulate fits well, for long-period purposes, with the fact that, according to the Trade Union figures, from 1850 to the outbreak of the first World War the percentage of unemployment over the average of good and bad years in successive trade cycles was approximately stable. It gives us one of the equations that we need; the quantity of labour at work is equal to an arbitrary constant. Besides this, Marshall also postulated, for the purposes of the *Principles*, that the general level of prices is held constant. He writes: " Throughout the present volume we are supposing, in the absence of any statement to the contrary, that all values are expressed in terms of money of fixed purchasing power, just as astronomers have taught us to determine the beginning or the ending of the day with reference, not to the actual sun, but to a mean sun which is supposed to move uniformly throughout the heavens ".[2] This gives a

[1] Cf. *post*, p. 29. [2] *Principles*, p. 593.

CONDITIONS NECESSARY TO EQUILIBRIUM

second equation; money income divided by real income, which is a function of employment, is equal to an arbitrary constant. The toll is thus made up. It need hardly be said that Marshall does not employ either of these postulates — to do so would be glaringly inconsistent with the facts — in relation to the short-period problems with which Keynes is dealing.

For these problems the two missing equations have to be provided quite otherwise. One of them Keynes derives from the postulate that the money-rate of wages is either an arbitrary constant or, as he once suggests, an increasing function of employment; a second from the postulate that the physical stock of money is either an arbitrary constant or an increasing function of the rate of interest. In developing the analysis I shall treat both these quantities as constants — constants whose values we are, of course, free to vary. But similar results follow if we allow either or both of them to be increasing functions.[1]

[1] Keynes claims that a scheme built on the Marshallian postulates would be embraced as a special case of his own scheme. What has been said will have shown that the relation is not quite so simple as that. We cannot get that scheme out of Keynes's scheme merely by making one of his variables constant. The two schemes are, rather, cousins with a common ancestor, both special cases of something more general than either. But that is an academic point.

VIII

THE CHARACTER OF THE KEYNESIAN EQUILIBRIUM

LET us now consider in a general way the character of the equilibrium, as regards employment, investment and so on, proper to any given state of the elements embraced in the Keynesian scheme. In that scheme employment in equilibrium conditions is not necessarily fixed at the level of precise fullness — in the sense that, apart from friction, everybody who wants employment always gets it *and* there are no unfilled vacancies. On the contrary, it may be less than full or over-full in any degree, according to the state of the various elements in the system. Unless one or more of these elements is deliberately adjusted to secure precise fullness, the achievement of that can only come about by a tremendous fluke. It is impossible to say *a priori* whether employment will on the average of equilibrium situations — *a fortiori* of actual situations — be less than full or over-full. We must not, of course, infer that it is less than full merely because there is on the average some non-frictional unemployment. Even with employment on the average exactly full, there would have to be some of that; because over-full employment can at best entail nil, not negative, unemployment. A decision can only be made *a posteriori*.

As regards actual situations that decision is not easy, because it entails a statistical estimate, not only of unfilled vacancies, but also of the average amount of frictional unemployment; and this it may be difficult to disentangle from other kinds. Still Keynes holds fairly confidently that there has always been in recent times a general tendency for employment — frictional unemployment being disregarded — to be less than full. He backs this view by reference to the inter-war experience of Great Britain and the United States (p. 219).

It may be that his view of the facts is correct. But, even so, his explanation of them is, as I think, misleading. For he seems to find this simply in the inadequacy of inducements to invest — in the demand schedule for investment being unduly low. Thus he writes: " The weakness of the inducement to invest has been at all times the key of the economic problem " (pp. 347-8). But it would be equally true — and equally false — to find an explanation in the state of any other of the relevant factors ; in the supply schedule of resources for investment being unduly high, that is, in the propensity to consume being unduly low ; in the liquidity preference schedule being unduly high ; in the physical stock of money being unduly low ; or, as, indeed, has sometimes been argued as regards the inter-war period, in the money-rate of wages being unduly high. It is by the interrelations among these several elements, not by the individual state of any one of them, that the volume of employment is determined, and, therefore, its excess over or deficiency below full employment has to be explained. In Marshall's familiar simile, all the balls balanced in a basin are equally responsible for the position of each.[1] Keynes, if pressed, would not, I think, have denied this, except perhaps as regards money wage-rates, about which something will be said presently. His concentration of emphasis on a

[1] Failure to realise this, or, rather, failure to adapt his language to it, leads Keynes elsewhere, as I think, into an equally one-sided statement : " The rate of interest is not the price which brings into equilibrium the demand for resources to invest and the readiness to abstain from present consumption. It is the price which equilibrates the desire to hold wealth in the form of cash with the available quantity of cash " (p. 167). In my view the rate of interest is the price that equilibrates *both* these pairs of quantities.

single element was due to his practical preoccupations; he regarded that element as the one over which there is best hope of exercising socially useful control.

IX

DIFFERENCES BETWEEN SHORT-PERIOD EQUILIBRIUM SITUATIONS

I SHALL now try to describe the ways in which employment, investment and so on will differ as between situations in short-period equilibrium when one or another of certain principal governing factors differs, while all the others are alike. In doing this I shall suppose that, as between these situations, differences of employment are equivalent to differences in the degree to which full employment is approached. In so far as differences in one or another governing factor affects the number of would-be employees — more strictly the size of the available labour force — that will not be true.[1] But to bring this into account would entail much verbiage, while the error involved in ignoring it is probably not large. The factors to be considered are the demand schedule for resources to invest, the supply schedule of resources to invest, the liquidity preference schedule, the physical stock

---

[1] Cf. *ante*, p. 23.

of money and the money-rate of wages. I shall suppose that employment is not over-full in any of the situations to be compared, so that our analysis cannot break down on that account; and shall leave aside, as Keynes does, complications connected with imperfect competition, price control and rationing. Also like him, I shall for the most part treat only of a closed economic system. The discussion will follow the general lines of Part III of my book on *Employment and Equilibrium*. It will be simpler and more categorical chiefly because I am, like Keynes, postulating here a single general productivity function instead of two, one relevant to consumption goods and the other to investment goods. Even so, since the argument is in essence mathematical, it may, I fear, in parts be difficult to follow when it is stated — inevitably with less precision — in words, still worse when it is read aloud. Throughout this division of my lecture I shall speak of *differences*, not of changes. As will appear presently, though Keynes does not bring out the point, the *consequences of changes* cover a much wider range than the *implications of differences*.

X

DIFFERENCES IN THE DEMAND SCHEDULE FOR INVESTMENT

CONSIDER first differences in the demand schedule for investment. The part of the discussion that has chief importance for practice has to do with conditions in which there is no threat of the net rate of interest being driven down below zero. Over this field analysis yields the following results.

If the volume of employment were taken as fixed, a lower demand schedule for investment in situation A as against situation B would obviously entail a smaller amount of investment and a correspondingly larger amount of consumption. But in Keynes's scheme the volume of employment is not fixed. A lower demand schedule for investment will still entail a smaller amount of investment demanded. For equilibrium, therefore, there must also be a smaller amount supplied. Therefore, with the propensity to consume, and so the supply function for investment, being what they are, *either* the volume of employment must be smaller *or* the rate of interest must be lower in situation A than in situation B. But, if the rate of interest is lower, the income velocity of money must be smaller, and so also money income. This entails that prices·are lower and so, the rate of money wages being given, that employment is discouraged. Thus in any event, whether the rate of interest is lower or not, employment must be smaller in situation A than in situation B.[1]

This is the vital point. But analysis may be carried a little further. From the properties of the propensity to consume we know that, if and in so far as the rate of interest is lower in situation A than in situation B, consumption must be larger, but in so far as employment is smaller, it must be smaller. We cannot tell without detailed knowledge of the form of the function whether the first or the second of these tendencies will be dominant, and whether therefore, both being taken into account, consumption will be larger or smaller in situation A than in situation B. If it is larger, the deficiency of employment in situation A as against B will be smaller than the deficiency of investment; in

[1] If the income velocity of money was not an increasing function of the rate of interest, but was independent of it, employment and investment would be the same in both situations, with the rate of interest lower in situation A.

SCHEDULE FOR INVESTMENT

the converse case, larger. Thus the multiplier, as Keynes calls it, obtained by dividing differences in investment into the associated differences in employment, while it must in any event be positive, may, so far as general considerations go, be either greater or less than unity. In his view, however, the supply of resources for investment is only very slightly sensitive to variations in the rate of interest. If that be so, the multiplier will, in general, be greater than unity. The fair degree of stability exhibited by modern industrial systems suggests in any event that it cannot be extremely large. In Keynes's opinion, for this country it is somewhere in the neighbourhood of 2. But that conclusion cannot be derived merely from the *general* characteristics he has assigned to the propensity to consume.

So far I have discussed only situations in which there is no threat of the rate of interest being forced below zero. Can situations in which there is such a threat exist? On the supposition that people in the aggregate save — which, on our definitions, implies equivalent aggregate investing — merely in response to the interest that saving is expected to yield to them in the future, it is easily shown that they cannot. For when, as a result of the increase in capital stock

DIFFERENCES IN THE DEMAND

following successive annual investments, the rate of interest offered by demanders has fallen to equality with the representative man's rate of discounting future satisfactions, the quantity of resources supplied for investment [1] must be nil. At this stage, since the rate at which the representative man discounts future satisfactions must always be positive, the rate of interest also must be positive. But, with the supply of investment nil, the economy will have arrived at the long-period goal of a stationary state, and there, apart from the introduction of some new source of disturbance, it must henceforward stand. It follows that in every position of short-period equilibrium anterior to this, the rate of interest must likewise be positive. No question of its being nil or negative can arise.

But plainly the supposition that people in the aggregate save only for the sake of interest does not agree with the facts. It is certain that some people desire to become possessed of a stock of wealth, or to enlarge their existing stock, for the sake of prestige or security, or both. Hence the desire to save will not cease when the rate of interest comes to equality with the representative man's (necessarily positive)

[1] That is Marshall's investment, *i.e.* Keynes's 'net investment'. (Cf. *ante*, p. 8.)

SCHEDULE FOR INVESTMENT

rate of discounting future satisfactions. There are two possibilities. It may cease at a rate which, though less than the representative man's rate of discounting future satisfactions, is still greater than or equal to zero ; or it may not cease at any positive rate or at the nil rate. In view of this latter possibility, situations in which there is a threat of the rate of interest being forced below zero cannot be left out of account.

What will happen, then, if such a situation actually occurs ? It may perhaps be thought at first sight that everything will go on as I have described it, save only that investment will become nil, not with the rate of interest positive but with that rate at some negative value. That, however, is not so. The crucial fact is that money can be held at practically nil cost. It follows that the representative man will not desire to invest *money* at a negative rate of interest. Hence, where relative values are not expected to change — as in the equilibrium of a stationary state — he will not desire to invest *anything* at a negative rate. But he will still desire to save ; and aggregate saving is equal to aggregate investment ! It follows that his desire to save must be aborted. This means in practice that it leads to his withdrawing from circulation into stockings or savings deposits an amount of money equivalent to what he desires to save. He must go on doing this day after day, thus causing a continuing decrease in the income velocity of money, unless and until this process culminates in a new equilibrium. Arrest may come through the desire to save stopping because, with lower prices, the representative man has accumulated in money so large a labour value of assets that he does not care for any more. Alternatively it may come because employment, and so the labour value of income, has fallen so low that, in spite of a considerable amenity value in holding wealth, he does not desire to save anything. At that stage, since the desire to save does not exist, it cannot be aborted: and the consequential progressive collapse of money income, and so of employment, comes to an end. This is the new equilibrium situation whose approach Keynes feared. It is a situation very different from the one which would be reached if the demand schedule for investment were sufficiently higher — a very little higher might do — to make the rate of interest positive. It is likely to comprise a much smaller volume alike of employment and of consumption. It is thus a low-level stationary state. In Keynes's words, "Employment is low

SCHEDULE FOR INVESTMENT

enough and the standard of life sufficiently miserable to bring savings to zero" (pp. 217-18).

This possible terminal situation, which his strong telescope has revealed to us, Keynes regarded, not at all as an academic plaything, but very seriously. Other things being equal, investment, continuing from year to year, must presently lead to such a filling-up of the profitable openings for capital that the rate of interest is only just above nil, and a small further fall must start off that cumulative decline, which, on his assumptions, *may* lead to the hell which he describes. At the time he wrote Keynes believed that for " a properly run community equipped with modern technical resources, of which the population is not increasing rapidly " (p. 220), that hell might become actual " within a single generation ". This was, of course, before the war, with its massive destruction of capital assets. He did not claim that it *must* become actual, chiefly because, as we have seen, long-period equilibrium *might* establish itself before the rate of interest had fallen to zero, and in that case a high-level, not a low-level, stationary state would emerge. But it *may* become actual. Since, however, there is every reason to expect that scientific discoveries will continue to be made, and so that new openings for profitable investment will appear in the future, as they have in the past, it may well be that no stationary state of any kind, neither heaven nor hell, will ever be attained ; but economic man for the remainder of his career will continue rather to live and move in purgatory.[1]

[1] When the stock of capital is gradually increasing in consequence of an accumulation of annual investments, even though no invention creates new openings for capital, it may happen on occasion that the demand schedule for capital, which, if people's expectations of profit were correct, would then necessarily be falling, is, nevertheless, pushed up on account of an error of optimism; with the result that the rate of interest, instead of progressively falling, rises. Let us suppose that the error is pronounced and that employment is over-full. When presently the error of optimism is exposed — as must happen unless it is bolstered up by continuing inflation — an error of pessimism may be induced and investment diminished below what is necessary to sustain full employment. This is the more likely to happen the stronger the error of optimism is and the longer it is allowed to last. In the initial situation the rate of interest is already too high, in the sense that, if it were maintained and the error of optimism at the same time corrected, employment would be brought down to less than full. Nevertheless, it is desirable to destroy the error of optimism, or, better still, to nip it in the bud. The traditional way to accomplish this is for the banks to restrict credit, thus forcing the rate of interest still higher. Keynes, in the course of a skilful discussion of this situation, is tempted into a paradox, though he qualifies it in a footnote, " The remedy for a boom is not a higher rate of interest, but a lower rate of interest " (p. 322). The truth seems to be, as earlier writers, *e.g.* Bagehot, were well aware, that a Central Bank policy directed to force up the rate of interest substantially may be desirable to cure the fever, but, when the fever is cured, the Banks' pressure should at once be released. There can be little doubt that after the 1920 boom had broken this pressure was maintained too long.

XI

DIFFERENCES IN THE SUPPLY SCHEDULE FOR INVESTMENT

SECONDLY, consider differences in the supply schedule for investment. This schedule is a derivative of the propensity to consume, which, it will be remembered, I am treating as a function of employment *and* the rate of interest. Suppose that it is lower in situation A than in situation B, so that there is greater thriftiness in respect of any given combination of quantity of employment and rate of interest. If employment is fixed at the same level in the two situations, it is obvious that consumption must be smaller and investment correspondingly larger in situation A, and that the rate of interest must be lower. But in Keynes's scheme, where employment is not fixed, the analysis is more complicated. Since, in respect of any given rate of interest and of employment, the amount of investment supplied is larger in situation A than in situation B, for equilibrium, with the set-up I am using, the amount de-

DIFFERENCES IN THE SUPPLY

manded, and so the actual amount provided, must also be larger. But, if the amount provided is larger, then, the demand function being given, the rate of interest must be lower. This entails that the income, velocity of money, and so money income, must be smaller. This yet again entails that prices are lower and so, the money-rate of wages being given, that employment is discouraged. In short, greater thriftiness carries with it a smaller total of employment.[1]

This conclusion is probably, as regards its effects on the attitude and policy of practical men, the most important element in Keynes's teaching. Whatever the justice of his criticism of the 'classical economists', there can be no doubt that in the period of the great slump many people did believe that thriftiness, or economy, would merely transfer employment from consumption to investment, thus not re-

[1] It should be noted that the analysis here is not symmetrical with that proper to differences in the demand schedule for investment. For when, as between two situations in short-period equilibrium, the supply function is the same, less investment necessarily entails less employment; but when, as in the present case, the supply function is not the same in the two situations, that is not so. It may be added that in this case, as in the other, there could not be any difference between the volume of employment in the two situations if the income velocity of money were independent of the rate of interest.

SCHEDULE FOR INVESTMENT

ducing it at the time and ultimately, in consequence of the contribution made to capital equipment, stimulating it. They believed this, not merely as regards periods of over-full employment, when, of course, it might be true, but also as regards periods of slump. This was a gross blunder. Nobody doubts any longer that Keynes's argument, as I have set it out above, is not only correct on his premises, but is also applicable in a general way to the conditions of the actual world. There are, indeed, two important qualifications to be made in it. If business men at home believe that the country is going to the dogs on account of extravagant consumption, an economy campaign may restore their confidence and so cause the demand schedule for investment to rise. In like manner — to pass for a moment to an open economy — if foreigners with balances here hold a similar belief, such a campaign may check a drain of gold abroad, and so help money income. These reactions *may* be large enough to make the net effect on employment favourable. Thus it is not certain that in the first stages of the 1930 panic the Government's economy campaign was a mistake. But few economists would now deny that it was maintained for much too long.

The analysis I have followed so far affirms

that greater thriftiness both entails less employment and also more investment. This means that the multiplier relevant here — different, of course, in mathematical form from that relevant to differences in the demand function — is not positive, but negative. Keynes does not accept this. On the contrary, he writes : " Up to the point where full employment prevails the growth of capital depends not at all on a low propensity to consume, but, on the contrary, is held back by it ; and only in conditions of full employment is a low propensity to consume conducive to the growth of capital. . . . Our argument leads towards the conclusion that in contemporary conditions the growth of wealth, so far from being dependent on the abstinence of the rich, as is commonly supposed, is more likely to be impeded by it " (p. 373).

From this he draws an important inference. In his view it is probable — and later statistical enquiries have confirmed this — that better-to-do people save, not merely a larger absolute amount, but a larger proportionate amount, of their income than poorer persons. This entails that a more even distribution of a given aggregate income would carry with it a lower propensity to consume — that is, less thriftiness. Now it has often been argued that large in-

SCHEDULE FOR INVESTMENT

equalities of income, however objectionable they may be for other reasons, do at least promote investment. But, according to Keynes's thesis, except where employment is over-full, on account, for example, of a war, or is rendered constant by a deliberate State or banking policy, the opposite of this is true. Hence, as he writes: " One of the chief social justifications of great inequality of wealth is therefore removed " (p. 373).

These conclusions are challenging ones. But they are incompatible with my analysis. For, according to that analysis, it is only through the fact that investment is increased that the fall in the rate of interest, which indirectly causes employment to contract, is brought about. The explanation is that, as I said earlier, Keynes regards the demand for investment, not only as a decreasing function of the rate of interest, but also as an increasing function of current consumption, and so of current income as valued in labour. If this was in fact so, and if the relation between income and investment demanded was sufficiently intense, a lower level of income due to diminished thriftiness would be associated with *smaller* investment, and, nevertheless, the rate of interest, which *must* be smaller if employment is to be smaller, would

DIFFERENCES IN SUPPLY SCHEDULE

in fact be smaller. In these conditions Keynes's conclusions would hold good. I have, however, argued earlier that, as between situations in short-period equilibrium, the quantity of investment demanded is not in any degree an increasing function of current consumption. If I am right, the assumption on which Keynes bases his challenging conclusions is inconsistent with the facts, and, consequently, those conclusions break down. But his *main* conclusion, that, in the conditions contemplated, thriftiness damages employment, is in no way weakened.

XII

DIFFERENCES IN THE LIQUIDITY PREFERENCE SCHEDULE

THIRDLY, consider differences, as between situations A and B, in the liquidity preference schedule; that is, in the proportion of their income that people choose to hold in the form of physical money at various rates of interest. In Keynes's scheme a lower liquidity preference schedule entails a larger income velocity of money; therefore more money income; therefore higher prices, and therefore, the money-rate of wages being given, more employment. This extra employment, carrying with it extra income, as valued in labour, entails in turn a larger amount of investment supplied and engaged. The implications for employment and investment are thus the same as those of a higher demand schedule for investment. At the same time the extra employment and the lower rate of interest associated with it both make on the side of supply for larger consumption. Thus employment is larger to a greater extent than investment is. This means that the multiplier relevant here — this multiplier is not mathematically of the same form either as the one relevant to variations in the demand for investment or as that relevant to variations in the supply of it — must be greater than unity.

XIII

DIFFERENCES IN THE STOCK OF MONEY

As regards differences in the physical stock of money it is obvious that, other things being equal, the reactions on employment and so on are exactly the same as those of differences in the liquidity preference schedule.

XIV

DIFFERENCES IN THE MONEY-RATE OF WAGES

THERE remain to be considered differences in the money-rate of wages. Everybody knows that, if in a single industry the money-rate of wages goes up or down, employment, provided that initially it is not "sufficiently over-full", will normally go down or up. But, as Keynes rightly points out, we cannot step from this to the inference that, if money wage-rates in the whole body of industries go up or down, the same consequences will follow. For it is possible, indeed highly probable, that a shift in money wage-rates in one industry will affect the money demand for labour in others. Hence the problem must be attacked on a wider front. If the aggregate money demand function were unaltered by an all-round fall in the money-rate of wages, employment — in the absence initially of full or over-full employment — would necessarily rise. Will the aggregate money demand function for labour in fact be unaltered or not altered enough to reverse this result?

Keynes agrees that in an open system, constituting only a small part of the economic world, neither of these things is likely. For in such a system, with exchange rates fixed, a fall in money wage-rates must improve the balance of trade, so investment and, through that, employment. More simply, with an international gold standard or other analogous arrangement, a fall in money wage-rates in one relatively small country cannot affect world prices, and so cannot affect its own prices, much; the gap between its money wages and its prices will therefore be widened in such wise that employment must be stimulated. Thus Keynes acutely remarks: " The greater strength of the traditional belief in the efficacy of reductions in money wage-rates as a means of increasing employment in Great Britain, as compared with the United States, is probably attributable to the latter being, comparatively with ourselves, a closed system " (p. 263). Clearly then the fundamental problem for analysis relates to a closed system.

In my opinion the solution of this problem, granted what has been said about the character of the functions involved, is quite straightforward. If the money wage-rate in situation A is lower than in situation B, employment is bound to be larger unless money income, and so the price level, is lower in a substantial degree. But, given that the income velocity of money is an increasing function of the rate of interest, money income cannot be lower in *any* degree unless the rate of interest is lower : and the only way in which the rate of interest can be made lower is through employment, and, consequently, the amount of resources supplied for investment being larger. It follows that employment is bound to be larger in the situation where the rate of money wages is lower ; and so also is the volume of investment. Thus the implications of a lower value of money wages are the same as those of a larger income velocity of money, that is to say, of a lower schedule of liquidity preference. Indeed, without this detailed argument, it is obvious *a priori* that they must be ; just as it is obvious that the same differences will be made to the quantity of tea bought if its price is halved as if twice as much is spent on buying it. I do not think — though I am not sure — that Keynes would have denied this conclusion on the premises given. But in his chapter 19 he introduces other factors, connected with expectations, not comprised in his formal set-up, which in some circumstances would reverse it. I shall be saying something about that presently.

XV

COMBINED DIFFERENCES

HAVING now examined separately the implications of differences in each of the several elements that Keynes distinguished in the key passage that I quoted earlier, we have next to observe that in real life these elements do not always, or indeed often, move one at a time. There are disturbances which act on several of the governing factors together. Thus, when people decide to consume less, this decision is often accompanied by a decision to make their position more liquid, which implies reducing the income velocity of money. Again optimism is liable at once to make the demand schedule for investment high and the liquidity preference schedule low. Nor need these effects necessarily be exactly synchronised. Keynes, for example, in his chapter about the trade cycle, expresses the view that " liquidity preference, except those manifestations of it which are associated with increasing trade and speculation, does not increase until *after* the collapse in the marginal efficiency of capital " (p. 316). Again a difference in one of our factors may, either directly or through the medium of associated expectations, *cause* differences in one or more of the others. Thus a high demand schedule for investment or a low liquidity preference schedule, leading directly to high employment, may thereby cause work-people to demand (successfully) high money-rates of wages. *Per contra* a large physical stock of money, as we shall see presently, in some conditions causes the liquidity preference schedule to be high, in others to be low. Thus, on the one hand, in times of depression the creation of new money makes the income velocity of money low (cf. p. 172); and, on the other, in periods of inflation it makes it high, thus causing money income to expand much more than in proportion to the physical stock of money. In attempts to explain actual happenings by means of Keynes's apparatus these interrelations and reactions would, of course, have to be brought into account.

XVI

EXPECTATIONS

I POINTED out earlier that the implications of a difference in one or other of our governing factors is by no means the same thing as the consequences of a change in it. Let us postpone for the moment the complicating fact that the responses of the economic system to stimuli take time to emerge fully. There still remains an important point connected with expectations. When two systems in short-period equilibrium differ as regards either the money-rate of wages or the physical stock of money, it is natural to suppose that in each of them the ruling wage-rate or the ruling stock of money is expected to remain what it is. But, if either of these elements *changes*, the fact of change is almost certain to carry with it an expectation of some further change either in the same or in the opposite direction. Any such expectation naturally has its own independent effect upon employment, and, until this has been taken into account, the full implications of the change are not known. To forecast the effect of changes in the money-rate of wages or the physical stock of money, we need, therefore, in addition to the analysis whose lines we have sketched out, (i) a further analysis of the implications of various sorts of expectation and (ii) some knowledge, or reasonable guess, about what expectations the change we are studying is likely to generate.

If the money-rate of wages is reduced and this causes people to believe that it will presently be reduced still further, buyers of goods and of labour alike will naturally hold back from purchases that are not immediately urgent, in the hope of getting better terms later on. They will be more anxious than before to hold money instead of using it. Thus the expectation of a future fall in the money-rate of wages raises the liquidity preference schedule, *i.e.* reduces the income velocity of money, and so lowers money income; and this may partly, completely, or more than completely offset the consequences of the actual change in the money-rate of wages. Of course, if the expectation generated is that money wage-rates will presently rise again, the effect on employment and so on of the actual change will be not mitigated or reversed, but accentuated. The other type of expectation is, however, at least as likely to

EXPECTATIONS

be generated. If it is, we can have no assurance that a general policy of cutting down money wages, when employment shows signs of falling, in order to prevent or check the fall, and of raising them in opposite conditions would achieve its purpose. As Keynes observes, it would certainly make for instability of prices. It need not make for stability of employment. Thus to hold, as what I said earlier suggests, that, in the absence of reactions on people's expectations about future wage-rates, lower rates must be associated with more employment is not inconsistent with Keynes's view (p. 269) that in the actual world they would quite likely be associated with less.

As regards the physical stock of money, we are on ground where more factual experience is available. In the earlier stages of the German inflation after the first World War it was generally expected that the upswing of prices and worsening of exchange rates there would presently be reversed. This expectation had the effect of raising the schedule of liquidity preference, *i.e.* of lowering the income velocity of money, with the result that money income rose much less than in proportion to the expansion in the physical stock of money. The consequences for employment of this expansion were thus mitigated by the expectation that was associated with it. On the other hand, in the later stages of the inflation the actual expansion in the physical stock of money gave rise to and was associated with an expectation that further expansions would take place. This expectation caused the income velocity of money to rise, with the result that money income increased much *more* rapidly than the physical stock of money. The consequences of that expansion were thus aggravated by the expectation associated with it.

In the two cases just described we could, if we wished, construct a set of formulae to show the implications for employment and so on of differences in expected conditions, analogous to the set we have constructed for differences in actual conditions. But, until we can discover some general principles for determining what sorts of differences in expectations are likely to be induced by given differences in facts, that would be of little practical use. No such general principles have been discovered yet. There is no technique for determining what assumptions are likely to be appropriate in different conditions. The best we can do is to look at each situation on its merits, call to mind what we have seen or heard about more or less similar situations in the past — and guess!

XVII

THE STATE AND INVESTMENT

THIS lack of assurance about the way in which variations in money wage-rates and in the stock of money will react in creating expectations about future changes discouraged Keynes from pinning his hopes on State or other action in respect of either of these elements by itself. Having at one time been an advocate of monetary measures as a chief way of controlling employment, he came, in the *General Theory*, to look rather to State action directed to control the level of investment. " I conceive ", he wrote, "that a somewhat comprehensive socialisation of investment will prove the only means of securing an approximation to full employment ; though this need not exclude all manner of compromises and devices by which public authority will co-operate with private initiative" (p. 378). If necessary, the State should enforce or induce sorts of investment that yield no fruits whatever. It is better — though, of course, still bad — that a moderate number of men should be engaged in digging holes and filling them up again than that a large number should be unemployed (cf. p. 220). *Prima facie*, State action that pushed the demand schedule for investment upwards would increase employment. Of course, by this I mean pushing aggregate investment, not merely State investment, upwards. It must always be borne in mind that investment made whether by the State itself or under the influence of State bounties, if it were undertaken in fields where private investors were accustomed to operate, would entail a falling-off of investment by them ; and this reaction *might* be carried so far that aggregate investment was hardly increased at all. With the State standing in the main outside industry, it may not be able to find ways of intervening whose efficacy is not seriously weakened by this kind of reaction. Plainly, however, in an economy where State investment normally constitutes a large part of the whole, this difficulty will be comparatively unimportant. With the State as sole investor it would disappear altogether.

It must be understood, however, that State action of this character, if it is financed by taking in taxes money that private persons would otherwise have themselves devoted either to investment or to the purchase of consumption goods, will not accomplish its purpose. It must be accompanied by the creation of new money, mainly, we may presume, in the form of bank credit. In fact a State investment policy directed to improve employment is, perhaps, best thought of as a supplement to an upward shift in the physical stock of money — a supplement that will prevent that upward shift from cancelling itself out by setting up an inverse downward shift in the income velocity of money. So interpreted, we may, I think, agree that, if our objective is continuous ' full employment' *and nothing else*, State control over investment offers, *for a closed system*, a more promising approach than any other that is open to us.

But what of the step from a closed system to an open one — particularly to one in which, as in Great Britain, international business relations play a very important part? Employment here is often threatened by contractions in the foreign demand for our exports; which, in the first instance, cut down employment in our export industries. Granted adequate mobility of labour out of the export industries, an expansion of investment at home might be used to offset this contraction, just as it might be if the contraction were due to an internal cause.

But that would not correct the excess of imports over exports, which the contraction of foreign demand must in the first instance bring about. There is thus a 'balance of payments problem', a thing quite alien to a closed economy. If the shift in foreign demand is short-lived, granted again adequate mobility of labour, that need not matter. But a lasting shift is serious. Clearly in such a case the Keynesian remedy would need at least to be supplemented by something else.[1] His closed economy analysis is not adequate here. But that is far from saying that it is not useful.

[1] Cf. Henderson, *The Future of Exchange Rates*, Oxford Economic Papers, January 1949, pp. 9 *et seq.*

XVIII

LIMITATIONS AND ACHIEVEMENTS OF KEYNES'S ANALYSIS

EVEN apart from this special point, and from difficulties about expectations, Keynes's analysis is, to my mind, very much more limited in scope and range than is often supposed. It describes what the short-period equilibrium position, that is, the position which is only not in full equilibrium because investment or disinvestment is taking place, — what this position tends to be when the relevant functions and independent variables are such and such; and it enables us to see how these quantities tend to differ as between situations in which one or another of them differs in a given degree. But what tends to happen when the conditions are such and such is not what actually happens whenever those conditions are established. It can actually happen only when the conditions have prevailed long enough for the tendencies associated with them to work themselves out. We are up against the fact, whose discussion we agreed a little while back to postpone, that the response of the economic system to stimuli is not instantaneous. Thus suppose that the demand for annual new investment, up till now low, suddenly becomes high. Then the rate of investment will probably continue for some little while at the level appropriate to the old state of demand, thereafter rising gradually to that appropriate to the new one. In a moving world, therefore, Keynes's short-period equilibrium positions are not the positions which are at all likely ever actually to establish themselves. Thus they are on a par with the long-period equilibrium positions, always pursued but never attained, which dominate Marshall's *Principles*. It is wrong to suggest that Keynes is more realistic than Marshall, in that, while the latter deals only with tendencies, the former deals with facts. Both alike deal only with tendencies.

It seems at first sight to follow from what I have been saying that, *if changes in fundamental conditions only occurred at fairly long intervals*, there would be dates and periods at which what tended to happen would actually be happening; so that for these dates and periods Keynes's tendencies *would* be facts. But there is a lion in the path here. Strictly, all we know *a priori* about our equilibrium positions is that, in respect of any given set of conditions, *if* they are established, they will maintain themselves. This does not entail that they will tend to become established. It may be, for example, that, as with the celebrated pig cycle, actual positions oscillate from one side to the other of the relevant equilibrium position, not approaching towards it, possibly even swinging round it in ever-widening arcs.[1] Whether in fact actual positions will tend towards the relevant equilibrium positions cannot be decided in any general *a priori* way, but only after a study of the detail of particular cases. The swing of a physical pendulum progressively contracts under the influence of friction, but we cannot infer from this that the swing of a psychological pendulum will do so.

Having thus looked this lion ' boldly ' in the face, let us henceforward ignore him. Let us *postulate* that, if changes in fundamental conditions occurred only at fairly long intervals, Keynes's tendencies would in truth be facts; — the consequences of changes and the implications of differences would be the same thing. With that postulate, let us suppose that at one date a short-period equilibrium position A is

[1] Cf. my *Economics of Stationary States*, pp. 13-15.

actually achieved and that presently, at a different date, when some function or independent variable has become different in a given way, another short-period equilibrium position B, appropriate to the new conditions, is established. Keynes's method could then tell us, not merely what employment, investment and so on tend to be at the two dates, but what they actually will be. But it could not tell us what happens to employment, investment and so on while the system is in *course of movement* from one of these equilibrium positions to the other; what they will be on the intervening days or months or years of this disequilibrium. Thus even in the most favourable circumstances that analysis is a staccato one, adapted to provide, not a moving picture, but only a succession of stills.

These are very serious limitations — limitations of which it is specially proper to remind ourselves when attempts are made to apply Keynes's apparatus directly to the solution of practical problems. This is in no sense to 'attack' Keynes or to decry his achievement. When a man has devised a new way of tackling an unclimbed mountain, we may, indeed, regret that this way has not led him to the top. But for the effort which has advanced him *towards* the top nothing is due but praise. The kernel of Keynes's contribution to economic thinking is to be found, as I have already said, in the short passage quoted from page 246 of his book. Whatever imperfections there may be in his working out of the fundamental conception embodied there, the conception itself is an extremely fruitful germinal idea. In my original review-article on the *General Theory* I failed to grasp its significance and did not assign to Keynes the credit due for it.[1] Nobody before him, so far as I know, had brought all the relevant factors, real and monetary at once, together in a single formal scheme, through which their interplay could be coherently investigated. His doing this does *not*, to my mind, constitute a revolution. Only if we accepted the myth — as I regard it — that earlier economists ignored the part played by money, and, even when discussing fluctuations in employment, tacitly assumed that there weren't any, would that word be appropriate.

[1] When I wrote my *Employment and Equilibrium* in 1942, and again when I revised it recently, I had not read the *General Theory* for some time and did not realise how closely my systems of equations conform with the scheme of his analysis. I ought not merely to have spoken of him as a pioneer in this class of work, which I did in my Preface, but also to have referred specifically to the key passage from the *General Theory* quoted on p. 20 above.

LIMITATIONS AND ACHIEVEMENTS

I should say, rather, that, in setting out and developing his fundamental conception, Keynes made a very important, original and valuable addition to the armoury of economic analysis. Any economist afterwards elaborating or refining on that conception is, so far, a follower of Keynes. All economists, whether followers or not, owe to the stimulus to thought which his book gave, even to the controversies that it aroused, a very great debt.

XIX
CONCLUSION

You will understand that I have been trying here to make an appraisal — a more or less technical appraisal — of one book, the most important, no doubt, but still only one out of the many books on economics that Keynes wrote. If you wanted an appraisal of Keynes as an economist, you would need a lens of much wider angle. You would need to bring into account all his other economic writings, together with the immense amount of work that he did as a 'practical economist' in the two world wars. In the first he was a high Treasury official; in the second, economic adviser to, and negotiator on behalf of, the British Government — this last work done under the continuing handicap of ill-health, which, with amazing courage and tenacity, he entirely disregarded. He would rather, he said, wear out than rust out. If you wanted an appraisal of him as an intellectual figure, you would have to look still wider. You would have to recall the immense range of his interests—drama, painting, bibliography, college

CONCLUSION

finance, college buildings, farming, even the number of wives that a boar — I don't mean a human bore — has to have if he is to be kept really happy! Keynes would explain to his friends that the right number is fourteen! You would have to recall, too, his brief but brilliant essays in biography. Edwin Cannan once said to me that *there*, in his opinion, Keynes's greatest strength lay. Above all, as I think, you would have to recall his early work on *Probability*, a book path-breaking in some ways, still, in spite of some questioning of its philosophic foundations, of high distinction in its special field. If you wanted to go beyond the intellectual figure and appraise the man as a whole with all his human qualities, as his family, his friends and his pupils saw him, that were a still harder task. It is not a task for me.

>   Ah, did you once see Shelley plain,
>   And did he stop and speak to you
>   And did you speak to him again?
>   How strange it seems, and new!
>
>   I crossed a moor, with a name of its own
>   And a certain use in the world no doubt,
>   Yet a hand's-breadth of it shines alone
>   'Mid the blank miles round about:
>
>   For there I picked up on the heather
>   And there I put inside my breast
>   A moulted feather, an eagle feather!
>   Well, I forget the rest.

APPENDIX

WRITE e, r, w and m for employment, the rate of interest, the rate of money wages and the physical stock of money. Write also $F(e)$ for income valued in labour; $\phi(r)$ for the demand function for income valued in labour; $f\{r, F(e)\}$ for the supply function of investment valued in labour; and $g(r)$ for the income velocity of money. Then the conditions for the Keynesian equilibrium can be set out, in the simplest and most concentrated form, in the four equations:

(1) $\phi(r) = f\{r, F(e)\}$,

(2) $w = \dfrac{mg(r)}{F(e)}$,

(3) m = a constant,

(4) w = a constant.

It will be seen that the number of independent equations is equal to the number of unknowns, so that the system is neither under- nor over-determined.